MIRACULOUS TESTIMONIES

GOD IS STILL PERFORMING MIRACLES TODAY

RaShonda D. Jamerson

JamerSun Publishing LLC

CONTENTS

ACKNOWLEDGMENTS

To my husband, Cory: Thank you for always believing in me. You pushed me to move forward on the path God laid out before me more than I could push myself. You moved life aside to make space for what is in me. I would not have taken the necessary steps without you. I am a very grateful wife!

To my children, Cory Jr, Aniyah, and Jeremiah: Thank you for being my inspiration. As you have allowed me to encourage you to do all that God has given you, you, in turn, inspired me to do the same.

To my mom, Carmella: Thank you for always being my sunshine. It seems unreal how much you love me and how generously you give your love, encouragement and excitement. No matter what I do, you always see me as Christ sees me. And for that, I am eternally grateful.

To my dad, Lem: Thank you for being the first to teach me about how to set goals and make plans to accomplish them. You taught me to always be ready for opportunities. I listened Daddy.

To my mentor, Denise, my supporters and encouragers: Thank you for standing behind me and encouraging me to continue moving forward. Believe me, I needed your support. Every time you asked about how this book was going, it encouraged me to keep going.

Introduction

In my pursuit of honoring God, I find that it is important to love God for who He is and not just what He does. To think of who God is and His heart for all creation brings me comfort, encouragement, and excitement. As I learn more about God through studying the Bible, praying, and spending time with people who follow Him, I realize that He is funny, serious, protective, persistent, and so much more. I enjoy thinking about how He made us, how He loves us unconditionally, and how He is always so strategic about what He does. I love watching Him work! There are so many instances when I think of God and smile.

Life can make it hard to remember all the wonderful characteristics of God. We may experience sadness, loss, anger, or grief—and feel like God is not as wonderful as people have said or as impressive as we once thought. As a therapeutic and school counselor, I have listened as many clients grappled with their faith in God when they were facing difficult situations or negative feelings and emotions. My family and friends have shared with me their similar struggles. More often than not, these incidences may cause us to lose the ability to "see" God for the magnificent being that He is and, in turn, need to physically see Him (with our eyes) as proof of His concern. These moments, the moments when we need to see a physical reminder of who our spiritual God is, are precisely why I wrote this book.

God's spiritual presence manifested in physical existence is called a *miracle*, but God's miracles are not something we talk about often. Although many practicing Christians believe in miracles, there is an overall tendency to believe miracles are ancient, old-fashioned, or even mythical. Do you believe in miracles?

As science and technology advance, it seems people think less admirably about the miracle of being sustained or being healed. The healings that were once acknowledged as miracles seem to have moved from being a privilege to an expectation of science. In fact, some people get downright annoyed when doctors are unable to relieve their pain or when counselors cannot instantly restore their mental health. It appears as if the humility people once showed when needing help has now turned into demanded healing.

I am often overwhelmed, as my life is an ongoing miracle. I grew up in a household where healthy marriage, consistent parenting, and Christian service were hit-and-miss. As a young adult, I chose a lifestyle where I broke almost all ten of God's commandments. After asking God to lead and change my life, I now consistently honor those commandments. I have been happily married for more than fifteen years, and I have three beautiful children, in whose lives I am immersed. I have had the privilege of leading different ministries, including currently · teaching couples more about marriage alongside my amazing husband. I am also working as a high school counselor at this time, which God has graced me to enjoy tremendously. While these may not sound like miracles, they are.

Based on my upbringing and the decisions I made prior to asking God to lead me, I should not live the blessed life I live. My decisions do not equate to this moment; God has truly been gracious and worked miraculously in my life. Additionally, I experienced a medical miracle several years ago, which I will address in a later chapter.

I have always been fascinated with the miracles that are reported in the Bible, so much so that I asked God why we do not see as many of them today, like in the days of old. Then, I came in contact with Karen, who shared her experience of the miraculous healing she received when she faced Hodgkin's lymphoma. Hodgkin's lymphoma is a cancer of the lymphatic system, which is part of the immune system. Cells in the lymphatic system grow abnormally and spread beyond it, throughout the body.

Before I go on, read Karen's testimony of how God healed her, as I know it will encourage you to believe that God is still performing miracles today:

HODGKIN'S LYMPHOMA— INOPERABLE

Four years ago, I had a large lump in my neck. I was told that it might be swollen glands. The swelling did not go away. It would go down and would come back, no matter what kind of medicine I took.

My doctor referred me to an ear, nose, and throat specialist. For six months, he continued with the swollen gland issue until I finally pushed for some exploratory action to be done. I was able to get an appointment for the next morning. I had the exploratory procedure. The doctor said, "You have Hodgkin's lymphoma and it's inoperable." [Hodgkin's lymphoma affects over 600 lymph nodes in the body. It is typical that when one lymph node gets infected, it spreads all over the body. Karen's cancer stayed in one lymph node. No others were affected.]

I had the surgery [to attempt to remove the lymph node]. I elected to go through chemotherapy and radiation. There were times that the large bone pain was so severe that I couldn't even stand up.

Despite the pain I experienced at home, I just kept praising God. By the time I got through, I was able to run up into church yelling, "Glory to God." I was not in remission; I was delivered from cancer. I go in every two years for CAT scans. When I go in, I tell the doctor, "God has healed me, so there will be nothing to see in the CAT scans."

Every time I go in, the doctor says, "You're right! The CAT scan shows nothing. Everything is fine."

One last thing to all who read about my miracle: stand firm in your faith in God. Don't let doubt creep in; that would only be saying you don't believe in the word of God. Remember, God is on our side and still in the miracle business.

Karen Marion
Grand Rapids, Michigan

After I heard Karen's story, I felt encouraged and began to speak with more people. I discovered there are tons of miracles that occur in our day and time. That is when my journey of writing this book began. I decided it would be great for the world to know that miracles are still happening.

Miraculous Testimonies contains a mixture of two parts. One part explores miracles—what they are, why we need them, and how we experience them. The other part shares interwoven testimonies of actual miracles that have been performed by God. While you will read about the testimonies of those who have suffered physical illness or internal brokenness and have been healed, it is important to note that God is constantly healing everyone, including you, even if it is not the way you have desired, recognized, or even noticed.

As you read about the miracles of God, my desire is that you will be encouraged to believe in who God is and what He can do for you. May this book serve as an encouragement to increase your hope and faith in the miraculous abilities of God. Most important, I hope it helps you understand that God performs miracles because He loves *you* deeply. I also hope your understanding of His love compels you to love Him in return, reaping the full blessings of the relationship. Please understand, no matter what life brings your way, God will *always* do what is best for you!

Chapter 1

God's Love

God loves us tremendously! He demonstrates His love for us by making His wisdom available in the Bible to teach us practical ways to live life. God gives us the "inside scoop" on how to enjoy life on Earth. He waits patiently for us to acknowledge Him as God. He endures our self-centeredness, our desire to treat Him like a genie, and our frustration with Him when life does not happen as we think it should. He welcomes us into His family at any point, no matter what condition we are in spiritually, mentally, emotionally, or physically, as long as we acknowledge our need for Him to lead our lives.

One of the most profound ways that God demonstrated His love for us was when He allowed His Son, Jesus, to die on the cross for us. God's original intention for our lives was that we be spiritually, mentally, emotionally, and physically healthy. As you may know, sin (caused by our deliberate and willful disobedience to God) interrupted God's intention for our lives. Sin stripped us of the ability to live the perfect and healthy lives God designed for us.

God created all mankind and everything in the earth; therefore, He knows what is best for us. God planned to lead us in ways that would benefit us all, which means we need to follow His guidance by reading His written word, the Bible.

Adam and Eve, the first people on Earth, disobeyed God's guidance causing a separation between Him and humans, which directly opposed His intention for our lives. The only way for us to regain the ability to live eternally with God was for Him to send His Spirit, in the flesh, as His Son, Jesus, to Earth to be punished for our sins, receiving what we all deserve for not following God's way (Galatians 1:4; 1 Corinthians 15:3-4; John 14:6). Jesus, who was innocent and sinless, had to die to serve the full consequence of our disobedience to God. God loves us so much that He would rather sacrifice a part of Himself than to allow us to bear the full (and deserved) punishment for our disobedience.

After Jesus died, God proved His control over death and eternity by bringing Jesus back to physical life. God then restored Jesus' spiritual life by bringing Him to heaven (Luke 24:51) to live eternally with God; thereby promising if we believe Jesus died for our sins and God raised Him from the dead, then we will be forgiven of our sins and live eternally with Him. In other words, since Jesus received undue punishment, He relieved us of all our guilt.

Once we believe Jesus did this for us, we can then appear innocent before God. It is this appearance that allows us to be able to return to being in God's presence, as before, living with God, Jesus, and all who believe in God, forever. We can be assured of this by what is written in 2 Corinthians 5:18–19; 21. It states, *"All this is from God, who reconciled us to himself through Christ...not counting people's sins against them. ...God made him* [Jesus] *who had no sin to be sin for us, so that in him we might become the righteousness of God."*

Pause for a moment. Think about how wonderful it will be to live eternally in the presence of God. He loves us so much that He made it possible for us to live happily ever after with Him. John 3:16 says, *"For God so loved the world that He gave his one and only Son, that whoever believes in him shall not perish but have eternal life."* Eternal life with God is more awesome than the most amazing thought or feeling of goodness, love, and peace that we can conjure in our minds. Living in God's eternal presence is for those of us who live a life surrendered to Him. In fact, 1 Corinthians 2:9 says, *"However, as it is written: 'What no eye has seen, what no ear has heard, and what no human mind has conceived'—the things God has prepared for those who love him[.]"*

There will be no more sadness, no more pain, no more fear—only joy, freedom, and newness. We will hear sounds more glorious than we have ever heard. We will see colors more magnificent than we have ever seen. The beauty and light will be more breathtaking than we can consider. The free-flowing love of God will rule our days. We will joyfully spend eternity with Him.

Think of the love you have felt for someone. Picture the power of that love. Your love causes you to offer kindness and patience beyond what you thought you could muster. It can persuade you to sacrifice all you have. Love will make you vulnerable, exposing your true self to the one you love. Love can bring an astounding amount of peace and joy in times of turmoil and chaos. It helps you to forgive beyond what you believe you can endure. God's love for you contains this and so much more. His love for you is unyielding, overpowering, and overwhelming. When you feel this kind of love, you should feel compelled to respond with the same unending love. So, in Mark 12:30, when God says, *"Love the Lord your God with all your heart and with all your soul and with all your mind and with all your strength,"* His request is beyond reasonable.

Life's Circumstances

As you know, life occasionally brings unexpected situations that can make loving God problematic. What do we do, then, when we run into dilemmas that block us from loving God? What if our heart is broken or filled with pain? How do we love God with all our soul if it is tainted with mean motives, filthy spirits, or hatred? Would it be difficult to love God with our entire mind if it is consumed with mental illness, disappointments, or regret? Could we love God with all our strength if we are overtaken by disease, physical disability, or if we have just experienced a painful accident? Many people find it hard to love God *without* these hurdles. Therefore, it can be especially challenging to love Him while living *with* them.

When unexpected life circumstances arise, we have several choices in deciding how to respond to God. We can choose to decide that loving God is too much work, that He does not care or does not exist, leading us to give up on loving Him. We could decide to follow different gods, thinking they would treat us better. We could also choose to grab hold of a relationship with God or hold tighter and trust that He is allowing the circumstances for a reason. This, of course, is a small sample of possible responses and some of which many of us have chosen throughout our lives.

Oftentimes, we seek relief and pray that God will help take away the experience that is causing pain or discomfort. We make promises that we will love or serve Him better. We offer the idea of spending more time reading, praying, and helping others if He changes the situation to be more favorable. Out of fear or frustration, we make promises that we may or may not keep. A clear example of this is in the book of Exodus.

Moses, a prophet who spoke on God's behalf, asked Pharaoh, the king of Egypt, to release the Israelites (God's chosen people) from slavery. When Pharaoh refused, God brought plagues into Egypt on Pharaoh and his people. During several of the plagues, Pharaoh would say to Moses in one way or another, *"…The Lord is in the right, and I and my people are in the wrong. Pray to the Lord, for we have had enough…I will let you go; you don't have to stay any longer"* (Exodus 9:27–28). After the plague would end, Pharaoh's heart would harden; he would not honor his own words and refused to let the people go freely.

We can also be in a place where we ask God for strength to endure the circumstance. The Bible speaks about a time when the people who believed in Jesus were being killed because of their faith. Their prayers could have been: "God, make them stop threatening us. Drive them out of the land." Instead, they prayed, *"Now, Lord, consider their threats and enable your servants to speak your word with great boldness"* (Acts 4:29). Just like the believers in Acts asked for strength to endure, we can ask for that same strength and expect to receive it.

Everyone experiences challenging situations, whether they believe in God or not. In fact, 1 Peter 4:12 reads, *"Dear friends, do not be surprised at the fiery ordeal that has come on you to test you, as though something strange were happening to you."* Ask anyone who has endured an affliction if they believe you will be able to endure yours. They will undoubtedly tell you how they survived and share that you can, too. People who believe in God will help you by encouraging you to stay strong until the end and to continue loving God, even when life feels too difficult to do so. They have learned that *"suffering produces perseverance; perseverance, character; and character, hope"* (Romans 5:3–4). They've also learned they are not facing these challenges alone. God is right here with us throughout the entire situation. Hebrews 13:5–6 reminds us that God will never leave us and He is our helper.

Although life's circumstances can make loving God feel strenuous, they do not have to stop us. There are numerous times when we are strong enough to push through situations to give God the love He truly deserves, the same way we would do for family and friends. However, pushing through and enduring until the end is not the only way to get to a place where we love God in the midst of troubling times. In His providence, God allows us to experience miraculous healings to instantly relieve us of discomforts, revitalizing our love for Him.

Chapter 2

Miraculous Healings

Every September since our oldest son, Cory Jr., was a toddler, he would cough violently, sometimes to the point of vomiting—and it would go on for months. Wanting it to stop, I started out giving him cough medicine and turning on the humidifier. When those did not help, I would try all kinds of home remedies. The last resort was to take him to the doctor. The doctor was always convinced that it was a sinus infection and would prescribe an antibiotic. The antibiotic would not work, so he would then prescribe a stronger antibiotic. Typically, that took us to about December, when the symptoms would finally begin to subside.

After a few years of this, I began to think this was going to be the norm as he entered each new school year.

One year, his coughing had become so bad that I took him to urgent care instead of his regular doctor. The doctor at urgent care suggested that it may be allergies. When we followed up with our primary care doctor, he prescribed allergy medicine, which cleared the symptoms up so much quicker. We were relieved; however, we would still prefer that he does not experience such severe symptoms at all.

We have tried all kinds of "tricks" to prevent the allergic reaction from happening, as we are really uncomfortable about giving him medication regularly. We realize, however, that there is only so much we or the doctors can do. There is nowhere on earth to look for help, so we are praying and asking God to heal Cory Jr. miraculously.

When we are physically, spiritually, or soulfully ill, we look for ways to feel better. We go to the doctor, take medication, see a therapist, or change our diet and exercise, looking to obtain better health. We may exhaust all our options before we conclude that literally nothing on earth can help us feel better. This causes us to desire the workings of a miracle.

A miracle is a highly improbable, extraordinary, and welcomed event that cannot be explained by natural or scientific laws. When we experience a miracle, we feel encouraged, renewed, and invigorated. When we are restored to immediate good health, we cannot wait to tell everyone we know of our remarkable experience.

Take Mr. Mullins, for example. He shared about an experience that led him to look for help from a doctor, use medication, and then experience a complete miracle.

16

His excitement about his healing increased his desire to share his experience with others. Read his miraculous testimony:

MEDICATION FOR LIFE?

Approximately four years ago, I had an issue with my blood pressure. My blood pressure was running very, very high, unbeknownst to me. I was giving blood at one of the blood donation stations at work, and I found out that my blood pressure was 220/160 [according to the CDC, normal is less than 120/80]. The doctor told me to go immediately to the emergency room.

The doctors in the ER gave me some medicine, but it wouldn't take my blood pressure below 180/140. They were still concerned because I'm a black male [The CDC says black males have a greater likelihood to die from high blood pressure]. They were very, very nervous because I could have had a stroke or a heart attack.

It took about six months to diagnose what was really going on. They tried a lot of different medications, but nothing truly worked to bring my blood pressure down.

The doctor thought there was no way I should have still continued to walk since my blood pressure was so high. God was still blessing me to come up and sing with the praise and worship team at church on Sundays. I was still doing all the things I do at work, even doing daily tasks. I kept going, even without any medicines truly working.

One of the doctors finally sent me to a specialist. The specialist determined that I had an acute adrenal gland problem. The adrenal gland sends a lot of potassium and sodium through the body. It's hard to regulate it. We found out that there was a tumor on a little strand of adrenal gland, and it was cancer.

The Lord really sustained me through that whole process on a daily basis. Many can testify that you wouldn't have known that anything was even wrong with me unless somebody told you. They were saying with a blood pressure like 220/160 that I should have been in a coma.

I feel it had to be the Lord sustaining me. The lady in the emergency room would tell me I was lucky. I would tell her, "No, I'm a blessed man because God was sustaining me until the problem was diagnosed."

They had to remove my adrenal gland. The doctor told me, "You're going to have to be on medicine the rest of your life because without that adrenal gland, we're going to have to regulate your blood pressure."

Glory be to God; no medicine was required afterward! And my blood pressure is now 106/70!

F. Mullins
Grand Rapids, Michigan

Mr. Mullins had a satisfactory plan for maintaining his health with medication after the doctors removed his adrenal gland. However, before he could even begin the plan that he and the doctors agreed upon, God decided to intervene and regulate Mr. Mullins' body. He needed no medication after having the gland removed. That miracle could not have happened by the knowledge or hands of human beings. The doctors only had the ability to get Mr. Mullins to the point where he could live using medication for the rest of his life. Thankfully, God is not limited to what humans can do. God decided to do something more extravagant. God decided Mr. Mullins would not use any medication at all, which is exactly the miraculous testimony Mr. Mullins is sharing with so many others.

We saw earlier that a miracle cannot be explained by natural (or physical) law. However, we can see evidence of the miracle in our natural realm (or physical world). Inside our physical world, we find items that can be experienced using our five senses. If anything originated from *inside* the physical world, then people could claim responsibility for creating it, duplicating any work that has brought relief or a solution. This means there would not be miracles at all. There would simply be problems solved by mankind. Since miracles cannot be explained by our natural laws, they must originate from outside the natural realm. This is what makes miracles *super*natural.

Since miracles are supernatural, they cannot be created by mankind. This means they have to be brought *into* our natural realm from *outside* of it. The question becomes, who can bring something from the supernatural realm into the natural realm? The one who can do this must have an existence unbound by a physical body. In other words, they must be a spirit.

God is a spirit (John 4:24), meaning He is not physically experienced by human beings' five senses. As a spirit, He is the only one who can operate outside of our natural realm. The Bible says God created all mankind when no one else existed (Genesis 1:1). Therefore, He has the ability to bring something into our physical realm, from the supernatural realm, that does not already exist here; proving His ability to do what cannot be done here.

Healing, which cannot be seen, must be brought from the supernatural realm, where it always exists (Revelation 21:4), into our natural realm, where it cannot be created. Once God brings healing from the supernatural realm into our natural realm, we experience either the gradual or immediate and unexplainable relief of pain or suffering, which we call a miracle.

NATURAL REALM
(Can be experienced by our five senses, or created by human beings)
- People
- Science
- Medicine
- Techniques
- Homeopathy
- Ideas

SUPERNATURAL REALM
(Cannot be physically experienced and cannot be created by human beings)

Chapter 3

Love God With All That You Are

When discussing God's love for us and our natural response to His love, Chapter 1 noted how Mark 12:30 urges us to do the following: *"Love the Lord your God with all your heart and with all your soul and with all your mind and with all your strength."* This prompting indicates we have a choice whether to comply.

It seems when life is good, it is easier to make the choice to love God and anyone else in our lives. However, when life is challenging and we need healing, love may not be as easy to distribute.

You may wonder, as I did, "How does it even come about that we need healing in the first place?" After reflecting on my own life, I realized that one decision affected my entire being, causing a severe need to be healed. As I have told others, pulling on one string of sin unravels the whole garment of blessings.

Long before I met my very wonderful husband, I dated a boy of whom my father did not approve. Let's call the boy Billy. My father instructed me to leave Billy alone. I, however, decided to follow my own way and date Billy. Billy was fun and creative, but also "down on his luck". I felt with my influence, he could be someone great. As the relationship progressed, I found out there was a lot more going on with Billy internally than I could see or perceive. After about four years, not only did Billy's internal struggles begin to surface, but the impact his struggles had on me started to show as well.

During our time together, I recall having a dream of two men dressed in all white who were pleading with me to stop living the life I was living. They were literally dragging me away and telling me I would go to hell if I did not change. I recall feeling that dream was significant, yet I continued on in my own way. Without knowing it, my soul was compromised by my one decision to be disobedient to my father.

I spent several nights crying over Billy, the relationship, and even nothing at all. I could not figure out why I cried so much or what was even causing me to cry. I found myself experiencing symptoms of depression, when I am typically a happy-go-lucky person. It was later revealed that Billy suffered from a mental illness, which I know had a negative impact on my heart and mind. As a result of my disobedient decision, coupled with my poor life choices, my heart and mind were severely damaged.

Eventually, Billy and I started having shoving matches during heated arguments. This led to him punching me in the face. My physical body was in jeopardy and in urgent need of healing, all because I did not heed the instructions of my father. I finally asked Billy to move out of the apartment, which felt refreshing. But by the end of that relationship, my entire being was broken and in desperate need of repair.

Perhaps you can relate to some of my story. Perhaps you cannot relate to it at all. Either way, the goal is to provide a bit of perspective on how easily our heart, soul, mind, or body can be placed in situations that lead to the need for healing. We do not realize we can be one decision away from destruction. We could carry an unexpressed feeling of being invincible. We may think or say things like, "That won't happen to me," or "I'll get over that," or "I can control that." We do not comprehend the depth of the vulnerability of our heart, soul, mind, and body.

Love the Lord your God with all your heart...

We know the heart is especially sensitive. We cherish it. We are cautious when we share it. We guard it, sometimes at all costs. We try our best to protect it from aching. Still, with all our safeguards, there are times when things get into the heart that we did not intend to let in; then we find it hurting, broken, or maybe even shattered.

If we are not aware of what actually tears away at the heart, we can inadvertently expose it to situations that are not beneficial in helping us fully flourish in our ability to love God, ourselves, and others. While the following list is not exhaustive, it does provide some insight as to the types of situations that can cause a heart to hurt:

- We accept inaccurate beliefs about ourselves.
- We compare ourselves to others.
- We think too little or too highly of ourselves.
- We are mistreated by others.
- We hold on to unforgiveness.
- We ignore our own positive qualities.

If we leave our heart in any one of these situations for too long, we can nestle into unhealthy feelings and emotions, such as prolonged anger, weakness, or defeat, believing we have no mental strength to overcome adversity. We may gradually become isolated or mistreat ourselves and others. Since the heart is a part of our overall being, if it is left in an unhealthy state for too long, it can negatively affect our soul, mind, and body, leading to sufferings like being depressed, inflicting self-harm, or developing psychosis. If our whole being suffers, the results can be devastating.

In my counseling profession, the heart is the main reason we see people in our offices. Case after case involves situations where people have been made to feel they were not good enough—they feel they are not smart enough to conquer a problem, they are holding onto regret about a matter, or they are grappling with unforgiveness of self or someone else. These situations lead exactly to the sufferings listed above. Of course, this is not the full list of reasons why I see clients, but it gives some insight into the effects of a hurting heart.

Healing, however, brings the heart to a healthy state. A healthy heart helps us to think more appropriately about ourselves, not too highly or too lowly. It allows us to accept the position we are in, not for the sake of settling, but so we are content; it gives us the ability to work toward productive solutions in problematic situations. Additionally, a healed heart permits us to experience peace, joy, happiness, kindness—all the feelings we need to be at ease, internally.

When the heart is well, it is easier for us to experience love as it is intended to be experienced. It enables us to live a life free from the weight of the past. It equips us with the ability to forgive ourselves and others. We develop confidence, which increases our vulnerability with others, connecting our lives with theirs. A healed heart helps us maintain appropriate perspectives of God, ourselves, and others. Most of all, a healed, whole heart allows us to accept God's love for us and reciprocate His love, as His written word requests.

With all your soul...

The soul is a part of our being that we may or may not think about too often. We usually mention it when we are referring to one of two things: looking for Mr. or Mrs. Right (i.e., our "soul" mate) or discussing what happens after death. Beyond that, we do not tend to put much thought into the soul. That being the case, we may not focus much on how to protect it, strengthen it, or determine if it even needs any attention at all.

Whether we give the soul attention or not, that does not change the fact that it needs to be healthy. Since we may not always give the needed attention to our soul, there is a good chance that at some point in our lives, we may have participated in ideas or activities that have altered it:

- Have you ever had conversations that cause you to dislike, or even hate, someone or some group of people? Have you ever gossiped or talked about someone in a way that was not meant to edify that person? Are you unable to identify with doing anything like this?

- Have you ever participated in paranormal activity? Have you ever practiced witchcraft or black magic? Have you ever consulted with a psychic? Are none of those your thing?

- Have you ever watched a movie and been aroused by the activity of the characters? Have you ever wanted to hit something after watching a fighting movie or wanted to be intimate after a steamy romance? Are you not into movies?

- Have you ever noticed that you picked up a bad habit of someone after you spent time in their presence?

There are several activities that we purposefully or inadvertently participate in that compromise the integrity of the soul. As these activities tamper with our soul, they ultimately lead us to be disobedient to God's requests. In some instances, we may get so far into satisfying our own personal desires that we no longer feel God's promptings. At this point, it gets easier to ignore what God is leading us to do, which causes the soul to become too weak to choose what is right over what is self-satisfying. At the least, an unhealthy soul can lead us to experience anxiety, panic attacks, depression, fear, anger, or phobias. These are a few indicators that our soul is in desperate need of healing.

When our soul needs healing, we will find that the heart, mind, and body are directly affected. For instance, a person may cause harm to his own body in response to feelings of depression. He may carry anger or unforgiveness toward someone, causing a broken heart. Another person may not eat or sleep regularly, causing a physical illness to begin in her body. She may cut or burn herself or even attempt, or complete, suicide in an effort to relieve the pain her soul is experiencing. Yet, another person may opt to have illicit relationships, causing their body to be negatively impacted by diseases or death and their heart to be riddled with guilt.

An unhealthy soul can position us to make decisions that we would normally deem unconscionable. It can also activate desires that are unhealthy, creating negative feelings about ourselves, which can lead to isolation from others, even from God.

I once counseled a young man who carried anger inside. No one ever found the source of it, but those who knew him certainly saw the effects. He became physically violent toward himself and others. He made rash decisions that caused him to steal a car, which he crashed, resulting in a broken leg. I also encountered a young lady who began practicing cult-like rituals. She later began suffering from anxiety, hallucinations, and even isolation, as she decided her family wanted nothing to do with her.

Considering all this, the healing of the soul allows it to be strengthened so it can again lead us to do what is right, good, and healthy, according to God's ways. Healing corrects our desires so we can treat ourselves, and others, properly, both physically and mentally. A healthy soul allows the mind to be balanced, causing us to make appropriate decisions. Most important, a healed soul allows us to return to the state where we can receive God's love for us and return it to Him, unwaveringly.

With all your mind...

The mind is an important component of our being. It is needed for obtaining knowledge and wisdom. It is useful for remembering people and information. The mind has been described as a powerful tool that cannot be taken away. We use our mind to make decisions about how we feel, what we will do, and how we will choose to execute our decisions.

As we know, there are situations when the mind can become intentionally or unintentionally compromised:

- Development of mental illness or disease
- Brain injury
- Choosing to ignore important information or lessons
- Willingly receiving incorrect information
- Denying accurate information
- Use of medication
- Chemical abuse

An unhealthy mind impacts a person's entire being. Since the mind is a component of both the heart and the soul, it stands to reason that if the mind is unhealthy, the heart and soul cannot be healthy. As we have seen and will see, an unhealthy heart and soul will ultimately lead to physical damage of the body.

Mental illness can cause depression, frustration, or anxiety. When knowledge cannot be retained or recalled, it can become challenging to take care of the body. Repeated offenses may hurt our heart if we do not recognize negative patterns.

As a counselor, I have frequently witnessed what happens when a person's mind is unhealthy. I recall a time when a client started to develop a mental illness. This person started hearing conversations that were not actually taking place. The frustration of not being able to make the voices stop led to the desire to commit suicide, as it seemed to be the only solution to make the voices stop. Another client developed psychosis, which led to frequent desires to hurt and kill family members and friends. There were others whose minds were so

29

consumed with anxiety that they literally could not walk, yet others who experienced brain injuries that caused the inability to retain short-term or long-term information—the frustration led to depression and ultimately self-destructing behaviors.

From time to time, we may reject information or wisdom given by others. The lack of following sound advice can lead to making decisions that make life more challenging, causing one to carry regret or endure difficulties that did not have to be faced.

A balanced mind allows us to rest, have peace, and enjoy the freedom to learn. And as we learn more about ourselves, we take better care of our whole being. We are careful regarding where we go, what we do, what we put into our bodies, causing us to be healthier physically. A healthy mind allows us to have concern for and regulate the heart and soul, being more aware of what we look at, speak of, listen to, or think about. Ultimately, a healthy mind helps us see more clearly an appropriate response to God's love for us.

And with all your strength

The body we are in is the only one we will ever have. Since we can see it and feel it, we are constantly being reminded that it needs our attention; it needs food, clothing, and shelter. We may be really good at taking care of it, or not at all. Either way, our body demands our attention when it is not functioning properly because it is the "house" we live in.

Similar to how our heart, soul, and mind can need healing, we can also find our body in need of healing. Most of us have experienced this at some point in our lives. Outside of poor eating habits, lack of regular exercise, and risky behaviors, we cannot control when our body begins to need healing. Our body can suffer from the following:

- Diseases
- Illnesses
- Malformations
- Accidents
- Other physical sufferings

When our body has experienced any of these situations, it can become weak, losing its ability to function. In these instances, it may begin to compensate for one part by overusing or misusing other parts, which can perpetuate the process of the body functioning incorrectly. It then takes an intervention of some sort to correct the body and restore it to its original state.

If help is not sought, or relief is not provided, the poor health of the body negatively impacts the heart, soul, and mind. When a person is in constant pain, it can lead to the heart of a person becoming prone to anxiety, low self-esteem, depression, suicidal ideation, etc. An accident that causes disfiguration can produce feelings of fear, anger, guilt, hatred, unforgiveness, or unbelief in God. There are diseases that impact the mind, causing psychological disfunction. While not all listed here, the

31

effects from an unhealthy body seem to continue infinitely.

Most, if not all of us, know someone who suffers or has suffered from having physical ailments or limitations. While some maintain a positive attitude, others do not. I recall counseling a young lady who suffered from multiple concussions. The impact of the concussions led to depression and anxiety, which ultimately caused her to stop pursuing her goals. I counseled another person who was physically and sexually abused as a child and suffered from ill effects that included low self-esteem, self-mutilation, suicidal and homicidal ideation. Even with years of counseling and medication, this person could not get well enough to function in society in a desired way.

A healthy body, as you are well-aware, brings physical comfort. Healing gives the body the ability to use its organs and body parts the way God intended them to be used. We can begin to work toward a state of a balanced heart, soul, and mind as our body returns to its original condition. When we physically feel better, we start accomplishing more tasks, choosing healthier lifestyles, doing God's work (i.e., serving or helping others), and enjoying life more. Our heart, soul, and mind receive direct benefits from the improvement of our body.

People choose various routes to achieve healing when the physical body is not functioning properly. Some will seek medical attention, some will learn to cope, and others will pray and ask God to help. In the following testimony, Martha shows us how she relied on doctors to help heal her daughter, Lisa, but also how God has allowed Lisa's body to be restored and sustained:

HOLE IN THE HEART

Four days after my daughter was born, we were preparing to leave the hospital to head home. The nurse came rushing in, saying, "We have to rush your daughter over to the neonatal unit at a different hospital." Then the doctor said, "There's a problem with either her lungs or her heart. We've got to get her there, or she's going to die." I was blown away.

The nurses in the neonatal unit said Lisa had a hole in her heart. The valve going to her heart was twisted, and they had to put in a shunt. When we arrived at the hospital, there was one pediatric cardiologist that would be able to do the surgery. The surgery had to happen within the next twenty-four hours, but the surgeon was booked until the next day. They said, "We may be able to get her in. [The surgeon] has eleven people before her." Our pediatric cardiologist said, "She probably won't make it. Just prepare for the worst."

I remember telling the Lord that I knew I wasn't really living for Him the way I should have been, and I knew I had been "playing church" for a little while. I knew I hadn't been real, but I asked if He could save Lisa [anyway].

That night, we went home devastated. The next day, I woke up and started to sing a song, "I Just Can't Stop Praising His

Name." I knew I didn't know anything about *really* praising God, but I kept singing it anyway.

I went to the hospital that morning, and they said Lisa had made it on the surgeon's list!

They were going to try to get her in. It seemed like every step we took, God had somebody there. Lisa's nurse told me that the surgeon and the nurses pray for all the babies. I was so excited that these people were praying for my baby!

I was feeling good all day, but started to get down again when it was time to walk her down to the operating room. Before the surgery, they took her down for a cardiac catheter. They said she might not make it through the catheterization because her heart was just that severe.

She made it through the catheterization *and* the surgery!

Afterward, the surgeon said he wouldn't be able to do any major repairs until her heart grows, but he did at least get the blood going. She stayed in the hospital for six weeks.

The pediatric doctor was still such a downer. He said she would never be 100 percent. He said to expect her fingers to be blue and cold. He told me to expect her to not be able to run or do the things that "regular" children do. He told me not to set my expectations too high. At that time, I didn't know anything about trusting God, so I left the hospital with low expectations for Lisa's life.

My brothers had accepted God as their Savior. They started instructing our family about how to wait on the Lord's blessings in times of need. I went to work and was sharing with my coworker about Lisa. She started to share with me about Pastor David and Prophetess Donna [her pastors], and how God had been using them to heal people. I started to attend their church.

[At the next doctor's visit], the doctor said Lisa was going to be on medication for the rest of her life. I wanted to stay positive, but I didn't know what to say when people asked me how she was doing. I learned to speak positively about her situation, even though I was giving her medication every day.

When the nurses, or anybody, would ask, "How's Lisa?" I would say, "The Lord is sustaining her." When she turned four, we had to take her to Ann Arbor to do the surgery. They put a shunt in her heart and a patch over it. She came home and was fine.

Every time I would take her for a checkup, the doctor would ask, "Did she pass out? Did she turn blue? Does she have any seizures?" Every time, I would answer him with, "No."

After several checkups, the doctor said she didn't have to take any more of the medication that he said she would be on for the rest of her life!

God was sustaining her just like the Bible said! The doctors said, "She's four right now. Between the ages of eight and ten, she'll have to have another surgery."

She had no surgery!

They said when she turns thirteen, she'll have to have another surgery.

She had no surgery!

They said surely when she turns eighteen, she'll have to have another surgery because "we still have that baby shunt in her heart."

When she turned eighteen, no surgery because God has sustained her all these years!

The doctor thought he was going to have to perform another surgery to replace the shunt because the longest he had heard anybody having a shunt is eleven years. Lisa has had the shunt in for over twenty-two years!

The same shunt that she had as a four-year-old girl is the same one she has as a grown woman. God sustained her all these years.

Martha Shipp on behalf of her daughter,
Lisa Snider
Grand Rapids, Michigan

God has certainly been gracious to mankind by allowing us to have the technology to perform His miracles. The doctors did the work, but God allowed the surgery to be successful—and God has sustained Lisa's life. God has done this for Lisa, and He can absolutely do it again when He deems it necessary.

If you, or someone you know, has received a report from the doctor or has had an experience that has been daunting or too heavy to carry, I encourage you to share the burden with God. Ask for His help with the matter and watch Him work.

Chapter 4

God's Way

Have you ever been in a situation where you were unsure of what to do to resolve it? Have you ever thought you had a solution to a problem, only to find it would not resolve the problem at all? Well, look at what happened to a woman named Tonya, who wanted to prepare a nice breakfast for her friend.

Tonya had bacon frying in the pan when she left the kitchen to talk with her. She returned to the kitchen and found a blazing fire. To put the fire out, her instinct said to pour a pot of water on it. Little did she know, the water would only spread the grease from the bacon, splashing the fire beyond the stove. Fortunately, her friend rushed in, stopped her from throwing the water at the fire, and poured flour on it instead, extinguishing the fire immediately.

While Tonya thought she had a viable solution to the problem, her attempt to resolve it was not the solution at all. She needed someone who knew more about the situation than she did and could think more clearly to help resolve it. Similar to Tonya, we have problems arise that deter our plans. We believe we have reasonable solutions, only to find we had the wrong answers all along.

Most people plan to live happy and fulfilling lives. But when we get to a place where we simply mutter the words "I don't know what to do" in situations where we have no solutions, this is a prime opportunity to experience God's miracles.

God is so generous with His loving desire to help all of us. He even enables those who do not love or believe in Him to experience His miracles and solutions to their problems. Matthew 5:45 says God allows the sun to rise on the evil and the good. He also sends rain to the just and unjust. This means God allows solutions and miracles to come to everyone so we may experience His goodness, causing us to live a life submitted to Him.

While I would love to say everybody gets to experience God's miraculous solutions how and when they want them, that is not always the case. God's idea of a miracle and His timing can sometimes look very different from ours. He says so Himself in Isaiah 55:8, *"'For my thoughts are not your thoughts, neither are your ways my ways,' declares the Lord."*

In the following testimony, we will read about Tina, whose baby was not developing properly in the womb. Tina and the doctors originally intended for her to have a healthy baby. When the doctors saw the major birth defects that developed, they did what they could to help. When they discovered they had no solutions to the baby's problems, their final solution was to encourage Tina to abort her baby. She rejected the doctors' advice and prayed for God's miraculous healing.

When Tina's son was born, he did, indeed, have some physical limitations. This new mother needed God to help, as she accepted that He did not miraculously heal her son in her womb as she had prayed:

> ### "HE'LL HAVE SPECIAL NEEDS. YOU SHOULD ABORT."

While I was pregnant, the doctors saw ultrasound pictures that showed my son would be blind. [The ultrasound also showed he would] have trouble walking because his legs were not forming correctly.

The doctors wanted me to abort him because I was young, and they thought I wouldn't be responsible enough to have a child with a disability.

When he was born, he was not blind!

As he got older, we found that his eyesight was struggling. At the age of thirteen, he got glasses. He had a horrible astigmatism. The doctor never thought his eyes, even with the glasses, would ever reverse.

One night my son went up for prayer at our church. Our prophetess spoke to him and told him to take off his glasses because God had healed him.

That night, he took off his glasses [and could see]. It has been several years later, and he is still not wearing glasses!

We went to the doctor a few months after he took his glasses off at church. The doctor said his eyesight had improved. He said it was probably because my son had been wearing his glasses.

My son said, "No, I don't wear those glasses anymore!"

We have the glasses at home. My son doesn't want to throw them away because it reminds him of how he was healed. He sees just fine now.

Also, after he was born, I noticed when he started walking his legs were really bowed. He struggled to jump. He couldn't run. He could barely walk because he was struggling. He couldn't even put his feet together because his legs were so bowed. We took him to a doctor. The doctor said to put him on a diet and not to worry about it. [The doctor assumed his weight made it hard for him to walk.]

I decided to get a second opinion. The second doctor gave me two options: I could either let the doctor break both my son's legs or have [him] wear leg braces for a year and a half and break only the left leg. I decided to try the braces and breaking just the left leg.

Right around that time, I started to establish a relationship with God. I started asking the pastors at my church for prayer every Sunday. After three months of my son wearing the braces, I took him up for prayer, as usual, and the pastors told me to take the braces off.

I took the braces off and right there, his legs straightened out!

He was one and a half. He was able to jump. He was able to run. It was as if nothing ever happened. He could do everything every other child could do, which as a toddler, he couldn't. To this day, his legs are so straight.

I praise God about how good He is. I laugh because my son is literally a walking testimony. I would encourage everybody to just believe God. It is never hopeless when you have Christ. Just look not at what the doctors can do, but look at what God can do. He can do miracles!

Tina Rositas on behalf of her son, Michael
Byron Center, Michigan

As you can see, God's plan was that Tina's son be healed. He just did it differently from how Tina prayed it would happen, and He definitely had a better solution than what the doctors could offer. Just because we do not understand why God does what He does or the timing of it, we cannot hold Him to our desired way of doing things or our time frame. There are so many intricate details that God considers in making sure that all people (who exist, have existed or will ever exist) experience His loving-kindness.

We simply cannot understand every aspect of how God operates. It would be similar to a toddler trying to understand the decisions their parents make. Cory Jr., for instance, loves building and creating with all kinds of objects that most others see as trash or want to put in the recycling bin. He sees paper towel rolls, cardboard boxes, and used birthday streamers as contraption possibilities. One time, he could not get a strip of cardboard to stay secured to the wall so he could race a car down the massive ramp he created. After several attempts, he became frustrated, threw himself into my lap, and asked me to "fix it."

I looked over the work he had completed and saw a few possible solutions. I did not, however, "fix it" for him. Instead, I told him that he is creative, a strong thinker, and I was certain he could come up with a solution. He was so upset with me. He wanted the solution right away, and he wanted *me* to be the solution. But I left him to his project. I needed him to at least try, for his own sake, to help build his resolve.

Later, he came running back to me, crying and feeling defeated. I asked him all the things he had tried. When I heard his ideas, I concluded that he was not at a level where he could figure out a possible solution. He would not find the answer on his own, so I got up, went in his room, and "fixed it" for him. He did not like or appreciate my timing, nor did he understand what I was doing: encouraging him to problem-solve, observing his abilities, monitoring his response to frustration, etc. Similarly, when God moves His way, we, too, are not aware of all He is doing within our situation. We do not understand what He wants us or others to experience. We just want Him to "fix it" for us how and when we want.

In 2 Kings 5:1–14, there is an example of how it looked when Naaman, a commander of an army, believed he had a solution to his problem. He thought he knew the best way to be healed miraculously by God. We have to ask ourselves if we are more like Tina, who waited for God to work in His timing, or Naaman, who decided he had the solution and expected God to work when and how he wanted.

Naaman was commander of the army of the king of Aram. He was a valiant soldier, but he suffered from leprosy. Raiders from Aram had gone out and taken captive a young girl from Israel. The girl was made to serve Naaman's wife. The girl told Naaman's wife that Naaman should go to Israel to see a prophet of God to be healed of his leprosy.

Desperate to live, Naaman asked the king of Aram if he could go to Israel and find the prophet. The king allowed Naaman to go and sent him with a letter requesting that he get healed of leprosy. The king of Israel received the letter and was worried because he knew he had no ability to heal anyone of leprosy.

When Elisha, God's prophet, heard that the king of Israel was upset, he inquired as to why. Elisha responded to the king by requesting Naaman be brought to the doorway of his home. When Naaman arrived at Elisha's doorway, Elisha sent a messenger out to tell him to wash himself seven times in the Jordan River and he would be healed.

This made Naaman angry. *"...I thought that he would surely come out to me and stand and call on the name of the Lord his God, wave his hand over the spot and cure me of my leprosy. Are not Abana and Pharpar, the rivers of Damascus, better than all the waters of Israel? Couldn't I wash in them and be cleansed[?]"* (2 Kings 5:11–12).

Naaman had an expectation of how God should heal him through Elisha. When God's plan was not in line with his expectations, he became angry. He decided the healing would work better if he bathed in cleaner water; he was still trying to control the parameters of his healing. Fortunately for Naaman, he had someone around who could talk some sense into him. Naaman had a servant who told him that he would have followed the instructions if he were told to do something great, so he should also be willing to follow the instructions of something unexpected. In response, Naaman went to the Jordan River and did what the prophet said and, instantly, he was healed. The Bible says, *"[H]is flesh was restored and became clean like that of a young boy"* (2 Kings 5:14).

Naaman wanted to be healed the way he conjured up in his mind. He almost missed the opportunity to experience God's healing because he had a method of healing that he believed the prophet of God should have used. How many times have you passed on opportunities for emotional healing because the guidance came from someone whom you did not consider qualified to offer help? Or the physical healing required you to do something you did not think was necessary? Or the soulful healing did not happen in, what you would consider, a miraculous way? If it is truly a miraculous healing that we are looking for, then we should be open to receiving it whenever and in whichever form God sends it.

Chapter 5

God Heals By Using People

God is the source of everything we need, yet He set up our lives so we could depend on the help of others. If we consider common phrases like, "It takes a village to raise a child," or "No man is an island," they show a general belief that we are not meant to live or function alone. In fact, if we examine everyone we know, we see that no one can live on this earth as a stand-alone person. Everyone depends on someone for something to function in this world. Think about it: who made the clothes you are wearing? Who prepared the medicines you use? Who prepared the food you cook? Who built the housing where you live? Everything we use, in order to live, has been dependent upon the work of others.

We saw an earlier example when God used the prophet Elisha to heal Naaman. Other examples are included in the books of Matthew and Acts:

- *"He called his twelve disciples to him and gave them authority to drive out evil spirits and to heal every disease and sickness"* (Matthew 10:1).

- *"Then Peter said, 'Silver or gold I do not have, but what I have I give you. In the name of Jesus Christ of Nazareth, walk.' Taking him by the right hand, he helped him up, and instantly the man's feet and ankles became strong. He jumped to his feet and began to walk. Then he went with them into the temple courts, walking and jumping, and praising God"* (Acts 3:6–8).

In the following testimony, you will see how I had to depend on God's people to help heal me. It was not something I could have done on my own (and believe me, I tried). It was also not something that doctors were able to resolve. In this case, it was a miracle that only those who operate according to God's power could have performed:

HELP! I'M ALWAYS NAUSEOUS!

The first four months of the year started off with two car accidents (totaling both cars), insurance battles, and a long-term fight with my college for financial aid. Around the last week of May, I began to get extremely nauseous about two to three hours after I ate anything, from a cookie to a salad to a steak. I tried to wait for it to go away by eating different foods or eating different amounts of food. Eventually, I went to see my doctor.

After almost a year of experimenting with different medications and seven different doctors' appointments, I was fed up. The last straw was the suggestion for a colonoscopy.

On Thursday, January 30, 2003, I was talking with my friend, Tomika, and told her that I hoped the doctors would find something during the colonoscopy. She had a fit! She told me to only speak healing into my life. She reminded me of the God I serve and let me know that He is a healer. I knew she was absolutely right.

That night I had a good, long talk with God. I told Him that I did not know what to do. I was depending solely on Him for this one. I asked that if I needed to go to the colonoscopy appointment, then I would continue to feel the nausea. If I didn't need to go, He would relieve my nausea by Sunday, February 2 (three days later), and allow me to use my story of His healing as a testimony. (By the way, I don't recommend putting deadlines on God. That is where my relationship was with Him at the time.) I needed to know by Sunday so Cory, my then fiancé, could take Monday off to take me to the appointment.

On Saturday, one of the pastors at my church, Stacy, told me about some church members who had a clinic where they use the power of the Holy Spirit to heal people. I told her I would check them out.

On Sunday, I ran into Charlotte, one of the ladies who worked in the clinic. She approached me, explaining that Stacy told her about my illness. She asked if she could touch my stomach. I agreed and she began to move her hands around, touching different areas of my stomach. She paused and said, "Your sphincter is rotating in the wrong direction. It's supposed to move clockwise, and it's moving counterclockwise. This is squeezing your vagus nerve, and this is causing the nausea."

She told me the doctors would not have found anything with the procedures they suggested because they were checking my stomach and my intestines. She gave me instructions on how to touch particular areas of my stomach and back to do some self-treatment. As I would do what she said, I could feel movement and hear a small gurgling sound.

The nausea was gone in a week and has never come back!

God used Charlotte to deliver my healing. I continue to thank God that Charlotte was open to receiving her gift of healing from Him. Also, that God used her to initiate my healing...Sunday, February 2!

RaShonda D. Jamerson
Canton, Michigan

God placed His believers in my path during the last few days before healing me. I needed each person along the way. Tomika reminded me to pray and expect God to perform a miracle. Stacy shared information with me about how those women were intentionally listening for God to direct them so they could help heal others. Then, God blessed me to be alone in the hallway with Charlotte, giving her the ability to identify what was wrong and how to fix it. Last, He allowed me to use my own hands to continue facilitating the healing.

Had I been like Naaman and decided the healing should have been instant or come in a different way, I may have remained ill and continued with many doctors' appointments. However, since I listened to the instruction given by His servant, I was healed. Could God have simply made me better on His own? Yes. However, He wanted to use Charlotte to do His great work in me.

It Takes a Village

We need each other to function properly on this earth. We depend on one another daily. We need human contact for mental and emotional stability. There must be human interaction on a regular basis to maintain a healthy existence. That being said, God purposefully uses people to perform His miracles to encourage us to depend on one another, rather than only Him.

Since God created us, He knows us well enough to know how we would respond to Him (and to each other) if He were the sole provider of miracles. While our possible responses are innumerable, this one stands to be highlighted—we are habit-forming beings who are drawn to the source of our provision. We tend to become directly dependent upon people or items from which we gain direct benefit.

God knew if only He performed miracles for people, we would begin to look to Him (and Him alone) for survival. On a spiritual level, we are to look solely to Him, of course, but since we are also physical beings, He wants us to engage with others for physical interactions and survival.

If we look at it from a parent's perspective, it would be like having two children. If each child looks toward their parents for interaction, that would be fulfilling for each child and disappointing for the parents. As parents, we want our children to learn to depend on us as well as each other. We do not want each child to deal with us only and ignore the other child in the house. We want them to work together, to collaborate, to help each other, and to share in the lives of one another. God feels the same way about us, His children. He wants us to engage with one another, walking alongside each other while on Earth. Could He handle each of us coming to Him individually? Absolutely. However, did He design us to work together and to help one another? Absolutely.

As we have already seen, I was dependent upon others to help with my sickness. Surely, I am not the only one who has depended upon the help of others. You or someone you know may have experienced healing through the hands of doctors or one of God's servants. You may even be someone who helps to heal others.

It is a blessing to know that God gives us the opportunity to help heal and be healed by one another as a reminder that we do not have to "do life" by ourselves. It is good to walk life's journey with others.

Similar to my experience with being healed with the help of someone, the following testimonies from two different mothers show how God uses people to help heal others miraculously:

ATTACKED WHILE STILL YOUNG

I had a normal pregnancy and labor. After thirty-six hours of active labor, they told me it was time to push. Suddenly, they said they had to do an emergency C-section; the baby's heart rate was not quite normal. I was really scared.

The doctors were able to successfully get my daughter, Brittnie, out. They did test after test and couldn't find anything wrong. They were completely stumped.

The doctors said they were getting ready to start the air med and were going to send Brittnie to Ann Arbor. They said they were going to put her in a machine that was going to take her blood out of her body, collect it, and put oxygen in it. They would shut her lungs down and give her lungs time to rest. She was a full-term baby and not a preemie, so they were wondering why she was having such difficulty.

My sister called her pastors and Sister Martha. I didn't know the Lord, but my cry was if He would heal my baby...just bring her through, I'll start going to church. I was willing to do anything at the time to save my baby.

The pastors came and prayed for my daughter. The doctors let the pastors take the stuff off and lay [their] hands on my daughter while they were praying.

The doctors said the air med was ready to go. We asked them to do one more test. They did another test, and the doctor came back and said her gas test was actually better. Her gas test was for the blood oxygen. They chose to do a thirty-minute standby. After that, they did another test and the results were better yet. Then, they did an hour standby. One hour progressed to twelve hours, which progressed to a day. Finally, they said she was not going to have to go into the machine that would take her blood out!

She was in the neonatal intensive care unit for seven days. She went home and was completely perfect. She has had no side effects.

She's active; she dances; she sings in the choir. To this day, she gives God the glory for being alive. It changed my faith because it was the key that caused me to start going to church and doing the things I needed to do.

Kimberly Day on behalf of her daughter,
Brittnie Day
Jenison, Michigan

YOUR BABY WON'T LIVE

While pregnant with my son, I went in for a routine ultrasound at five or six months. After reviewing the ultrasound, the nurse had a look on her face that concerned me. She said, "Oh, I'll be right back, Mrs. Day."

All of a sudden, some doctors came in the room. Then, some medical teams came in. They said they wanted to check on some things.

They came back with the pictures from the ultrasound and some big X-ray-like pictures. They said they were unable to locate my son's kidneys, his spleen, his cerebellum, and his brain. They could see all his other parts, so they believed it was not a bad picture.

They explained they were not able to hear all the chambers of his heart. They could only hear three of the four chambers. They said, "We'll see. But at the time, the cerebellum's inability to function would not allow the baby to grow. You would deliver the baby, but the baby would cease to be alive within an hour's span."

I was completely numb. I was in shock. I work at a church so when I went to the office, a couple of our pastors were there.

They immediately started praying about having faith that my child would be healthy. They started praying that this is a child destined of God and that this was a boy baby. We didn't even know it was a boy at the time.

My pastors just spoke right to the baby in my stomach, saying, "You are healed in the name of Jesus." My husband was praying with his hands on my stomach, too. It was a very difficult time for all of us.

When I went in for my next ultrasound, they said, "We hear four chambers of the heart!"

On January 7, my son was born, and his body was perfect. He is a ball of energy and enjoys running, talking, and jumping, just like all the other boys his age.

Kimberly Day on behalf of her son, Thomas Day, Jr.
Jenison, Michigan

SORE THROAT TO KIDNEY BIOPSY

"It all started with a sore throat that turned to strep throat. A couple weeks later, I got a rash from my thigh down to my feet. My legs had sores on them. My muscles were tightening. I had to walk on my heels so the sores on the base of my feet didn't touch the ground," said Aja, Cynda's daughter. "My mom took me to the doctor a lot. They could not figure out what was causing the symptoms. I went to a specialist. He recognized the symptoms and said I needed a kidney biopsy immediately."

"I was sent to a major hospital in Ann Arbor because the local hospital could not perform the procedure. I don't remember much beyond that. I do remember being on a lot of medication," Aja continued.

The specialist said he had only seen this condition once in his whole career; most regular doctors or dermatologists wouldn't have caught this.

While driving to Ann Arbor for the doctor's appointment, we hit black ice and spun 360 degrees. We landed in the middle of a snowbank. No one was hurt, and we did not hit anyone else. That was a miracle within the miracle.

The spinout caused us to miss the appointment. We returned to Grand Rapids that night. We had to take a bus to Ann Arbor the next day. We had our pastors praying for us.

The results of the tests showed Aja had a condition affecting her kidneys as a result of the strep. We were so grateful that God allowed the doctor to find the problem and provide treatment for Aja. We are also grateful that the doctor said she would be on medication for six months, but she was only on [medication] for two [months].

She has never had any health issues since!

Cynda B.
Grand Rapids, Michigan

Brittnie and Thomas Jr.'s miracles came by God through the prayers of those who believe in Him. So many of the situations we face can be foreign to us, leaving us without understanding or awareness that we can fight against them with prayer. In other moments, the situations we are in can be so overwhelming that we need the help of others to come in and pray for us or with us. Similarly, we do this when we seek our family and friends' advice or presence in "everyday life" situations, such as how to handle a problem at work, difficult children, or a change in direction. We depend on the help of others during times of grief and loss. In both cases, Kimberly depended on the prayers of others to help bring miracles to her two children.

Aja's miracle came by the hands of a doctor and God's favor. First, she had a physician who had only seen her condition one other time in his entire career. Her mother noted that most doctors would not have properly identified Aja's condition, but this particular doctor had. It is a blessing they happened to have been seen by him. They certainly did not know to look for him as they had no idea what caused Aja's condition.

Then, while seeking help, Aja and her mom spun out on the freeway without getting hurt or hurting anyone else. Last, Aja was able to get the care she needed and recover three times faster than the doctor predicted. While her miracle of healing did not come in an instant, it came nonetheless; and when it came, it came quickly with the help of their doctor.

As we see, God uses people to help heal others. People cannot heal people all by themselves. Doctors and nurses certainly facilitate healing through their knowledge, medication, and procedures. We must acknowledge, though, that while we are grateful for their care, it is God who allows their work to be effective.

Medication does not have to work. It can pass through the body without having any effect, no different from a mistakenly swallowed bead or coin that the body cannot digest. Instead, God allows the medication to interact with the body in a way that helps bring relief. We see the same thing when doctors perform surgeries, putting all sections of the body in their proper places; but the blood does not have to begin flowing again, the organs and muscles do not have to reconnect, and the body does not have to regain its function.

Counseling does not have to help people feel better, it is God who permits the words to be effective and the internal healing to take place. There is no healing on earth that takes place without the hand of God. Although some do not say it or even realize it, medical professionals rely on God to finish *all* their processes and procedures.

Jesus, while here on Earth, had the ability to perform several miracles of the heart, soul, mind, and body. *"Jesus did many other miraculous signs in the presence of his disciples, which are not recorded in this book"* (John 20:30).

Here are a few examples of Jesus' ability to heal:

- Jesus traveled to Jerusalem and as He entered into a village, ten men with leprosy met Him. They asked Him to have pity on them and heal them. Jesus healed them and sent them to the priests to verify their healing (Luke 17:11–14).

- As Jesus taught and preached the good news of the kingdom [of God] in the synagogues throughout Galilee, He healed every disease and sickness that the people had (Matthew 4:23).

- Jesus healed a demon-possessed man in the region of the Gerasenes. After Jesus healed him, he was found *"in his right mind"* (Mark 5:1–20).

- Jesus removed a demon from a boy who had seizures and multiple attempts of completing suicide (Matthew 17:14–18).

- Jesus healed a man named Lazarus from death by bringing him back to life (John 11:1–44).

We already established that God created everything inside and outside of the earth. With that, He made us to live according to our own free will, giving us the freedom to believe in Him and believe what He can do. Even though we are drawn to the source of our provision, because of free will, we can choose to decide if God, someone, or something is our source of provision. That being said, even if God performed all miracles for all people, some would choose to believe He was not the one who provided for them. They would begin to seek other explanations or sources for their miracles, calling them the result of their own knowledge, hard work, coincidence, luck, or natural consequences.

Since people have the tendency to worship the source of their provision, when God chooses to use people to perform His miracles, He does so with the understanding that it could cause those who were healed to "worship" the person from whom they received their healing. While we know worshipping people is not what God wants, He understands how we think and has, therefore, calculated that into His plan for revealing that He is the true source of their healing.

When those who are healed look to worship God's people (the ones God uses to provide the miraculous healings), God's people know to lead the healed person back to God. The book of Acts shows this exact point when Peter and John, followers of Jesus, healed a lame beggar. The people who witnessed this miraculous event looked toward Peter and John like gods. But Peter made it very clear that he was not operating in his own ability; he encouraged them to have faith in God since He gave them the ability to heal the beggar:

- *"While the beggar held on to Peter and John, all the people were astonished and came running to them in the place called Solomon's Colonnade. When Peter saw this, he said to them: 'Men of Israel, why does this surprise you? Why do you stare at us as if by our own power or godliness we had made this man walk?'"* (Acts 3:11–12).

- *"By faith in the name of Jesus, this man whom you see and know was made strong. It is Jesus' name and the faith that comes through him that has given this complete healing to him, as you can all see"* (Acts 3:16).

Whether in the biblical days or today's time, God is still using people to help others to be miraculously restored mentally, emotionally, spiritually, and physically.

Chapter 6

God Heals People Himself

Our son, Jeremiah, enjoys eating. He especially enjoys eating from different restaurants. If he could eat out every day for every meal, he would undoubtedly enjoy each experience. While Cory and I take the kids to restaurants on occasion, most times we want them to have food prepared by our own hands. We want to make sure they get the vitamins and nutrients they need through healthy and nutritious meals. We want them to be accustomed to the way we prepare food instead of desiring the food preparation of others. We enjoy making some of their favorite foods and watching the smile on their faces when they see their plate sitting on the table. I, personally, enjoy hearing Jeremiah say, "Thank you, Mom! This is the best meal ever" (albeit, he says that for almost every meal). Cory and I gain satisfaction in knowing our kids are eating and enjoying food we have prepared for them—food that is good for them.

Similarly, as we saw in the previous chapter, God uses people to help those who have ailments and illnesses. Sometimes, though, God decides to perform miracles Himself. When Jesus spoke, in advance, about His resurrection, He was not referring to a medical procedure that would bring Him back to life. Jesus claimed God would raise Him from the dead, which is exactly what God did. The following scripture is the statement from an eyewitness regarding the greatest miracle of all time: *"God has raised this Jesus to life, and we are all witnesses of the fact"* (Acts 2:32).

Jesus was not the only one whom God, Himself, healed. In the book of Acts, the Bible shares that Saul (later called Paul) became blind. After he did what God instructed him to do, scales fell from his eyes, restoring his sight (Acts 9:18). There was no eye surgery or any of God's people doing anything to help restore Saul's sight. God caused the scales to fall off Himself.

Later in Acts, we saw that Paul was bitten by a venomous snake. As the locals awaited his certain death, they discovered that he shook the snake off his hand and suffered no ill effects (Acts 28:5). God healed Paul from the deadly venom that the locals were sure would kill him.

When we slow down long enough and process our experiences, we will recognize that God heals us daily. He has designed our bodies to heal naturally and restore themselves. We have been built with tremendous healing ability:

- Rest eases our mind and replenishes our strength.
- Wounds heal on their own.
- Hair regrows after it has been removed.
- Eyes water and noses sneeze to flush out foreign objects.
- Coughs clear throats and lungs.
- White blood cells fight colds and other infections.

While we generally do not think of these functions as God healing us, we must admit that we do not and cannot control any of these actions on our own. If a person tried to "will" a wound to close, she would see that it heals no faster or slower than it usually does. If one strained to make his white blood cells multiply to better fight illnesses, he would find the cells do what they have always done.

Have you ever been in a quiet location and felt a sneeze or cough coming? How successful were you at stopping it? No matter how much we want to avoid sneezing or coughing to clear our passages, the body does what is needed for better health, *without* consulting us first.

We have become so accustomed to receiving these daily healings that we write them off as insignificant and expected. We take for granted our body's daily functions and how we are restored. We should all appreciate that God allows our bodies to heal without any conscious effort on our part, as it would require us to be preoccupied with restoration every moment of every day.

In some circumstances, God allows His built-in systems to malfunction and at that point, He may decide to allow miraculous healings and sometimes by His own power. The following testimonies are about miracles that God performed Himself:

BY HIS STRIPES, MY KNEE IS HEALED!

I slipped and fell down the stairs in my house; and I hurt my knee. When I went to my doctor, he said I would have to have surgery. I said, "No, I'm going to church and I'm going to have my pastors pray for my knee; and I'm going to be healed."

I went to church and received prayer. I thought, "*This is it. Somebody take these crutches. I'm fine.*" Lo and behold, I was still hobbling on crutches when I left. It got to a point where I could walk without the crutches, but my knee would still hurt...especially at night.

My knee would hurt so badly it would wake me up. The pain continued. This happened over a six-month period. I kept going up for prayer at church and saying, "Lord, I believe you. Why am I not healed? You said we were healed 2,000 years ago [referencing Isaiah 53:5]."

One night my knee hurt so badly that I woke up and I was angry. I was angry that the pain was trying to stick around. I had enough! I said, "I was healed 2,000 years ago. This is it." I began to declare, "Stripe number 1, I'm healed in Jesus' name." I was going to 39 [Jesus was whipped these many times before His crucifixion]. I got to stripe 16 or 17, and I dropped off to sleep.

My knee has not hurt from that night to this day. Healed! Healed! That was over 12 years ago!

God's word is true. If He says you are healed, you are healed. When He took those stripes across His back, my healing was secure. My knee has not hurt from that night to this day. I don't wake up at night with knee pain or anything. That is my testimony.

Martha Shipp
Grand Rapids, Michigan

God is sovereign, meaning He possesses supreme power. He chooses who He heals and how He heals them. We may or may not understand why He makes the choices He makes, but our understanding is not a prerequisite for believing what God can do. It is important, though, for us to believe He is who He says He is and can do what He says He can do. It is through our faith in Him that we position ourselves to be restored to good health. There are multiple accounts in the Bible where Jesus tells people their faith is what made them well, such as in Matthew 9:22 and Luke 17:19.

In Chapter 5, Cynda recounted how doctors helped her daughter, Aja, experience a miraculous healing of her kidneys and how God blessed Aja to get off medication earlier than expected. In the following testimony, Cynda and her husband, Henry, share how God protected his heart from two heart attacks by allowing there to be no damage at all. Only God can perform such a miracle:

TWO HEART ATTACKS AND NO DAMAGE!

Four or five years ago, my husband woke up in the middle of the night and went downstairs. All of a sudden, I heard a "boom." I didn't know what it was, but Aja happened to have been on the couch and saw her father fall down. She rolled him over, and his eyes started glazing over. She called me downstairs.

I nudged him slightly, and he jumped up off the floor and sat on the couch. He said his chest felt really heavy, but he would be fine. So we took him to the emergency room. I was not feeling well and did not want to get anyone sick, so I sat in the waiting room. I sat down for about a minute, and they called me back. They said my husband had a heart attack and that they were running tests and found that one of his vessels was 99 percent closed.

The hospital where we were didn't have anyone there that could help. We had to go to a different hospital. I called our pastors, and they had all of the pastors, the elders, and Apostle Dave come to where we were. We waited in the waiting room, and we prayed. The doctor came out within a half hour and said they were able to open the artery with a balloon-type item and he was fine.

The doctors could not figure out why he had a heart attack since he was fit and had no family history. They put him on medication and continued to watch him.

Within two years, he had a second heart attack. He was having a heart attack, but he was sitting up and talking. When we got to the hospital, the same team came in within an hour. This time they had to put in a stent.

With it being his second heart attack, they were concerned it would have done damage to his heart. The miracle is after the test came back, there was no damage at all.

After two heart attacks, no damage has been done to his heart whatsoever. It's been more than two years since.

You can tell this is a miracle of God!

Cynda B. on behalf of her husband, Henry B.
Grand Rapids, Michigan

The testimonies in this chapter are but a small fragment of the types of miracles God performs regularly. We should be encouraged to keep our eyes and ears open and pay attention to the healings that we experience or that we see around us. If we choose to acknowledge God's great work in our lives, we will see more of what He is doing every day.

Chapter 7

Why Does God Heal Miraculously?

W hen my children fall and scrape their knees, I do not like it. I wish for them to be well. If they are crying, I feel a little sad on the inside; almost like it scrapes my heart a little bit. This empathy causes me to look for ways to take care of their wounds. I clean them with water and peroxide, I put ointment on it, and then I cover it with a bandage. When the process is done, I ask, "How does that feel?" They almost always say, "Better. Thank you, Mom." They smile and may give me a hug. Showing my kids that I care about their wounds and doing my part to help in the healing process makes them feel loved and nurtured. It also increases their belief that they can depend on me.

My kids know I have access to materials and information about wounds that they do not. They do not understand how peroxide and ointment work or how to use them to feel better, but I do. They depend on me for help with healing, which is great because my desire is for them to feel better. I find joy in their smiles and their hugs—and I want their wounds to heal properly. I help them because I love them. I take pleasure in the love they return to me when they feel better.

God feels the same way about us when we are hurt. Chapter 2 briefly discussed why God heals us miraculously. While there are many reasons why He heals us, let's dive a little deeper into the following six, especially focusing on the last two for the remainder of this chapter:

1. *God loves us.* He says so over and over in the Bible, from the most commonly known scripture (John 3:16) to many others (Romans 5:8; 1 John 4:19; Lamentations 3:22). Just as parents repeat important information to their children multiple times in the hope that they will understand and remember, God repeats how much He cherishes us, which tells us how much He wants us to know and remember how He feels about us.

2. *God has designed our lives to have a significant future.* In the process of advancing toward our future, God understands that there will be times when we have need for provision, healing, and even miracles. As in the example of me helping with my children's wounds, God has access to materials and information that we do not. He

provides what we need because He loves us and wants us to have all the necessary pieces to attain the great future that He put in place for us.

3. *God wants us to be well.* He shares His desires repeatedly in the scriptures. Each time He gives us an instruction that leads to living well, it is another indication that He cares. When you give advice that you know will be helpful for others, what you are really doing is leading them toward living a good life because you want things to go well for them. Similarly, God gives instructions throughout the Bible that He says will lead to all being well with us. In Exodus 20:12, He gives instructions on how to live a long life. In Deuteronomy 12:28 and Jeremiah 7:23, He gives instructions so all be well with us.

4. *God is showing that He controls all things.* As covered in Chapter 2, God brings healing from the supernatural realm to the natural realm. This means He can operate between the two realms. This also means we can trust Him when He says what happens after death. As we look in the scriptures, we see that Jesus did not heal just for the sake of making life comfortable for people; He healed so people would believe He had the authority to declare their sins forgiven, allowing them to live eternally in God's presence.

5. *God wants to draw attention toward Him so you will believe.* He does not allow people to be healed solely for the purpose of feeling better; He allows healing so people will feel compelled to trust and believe in Him. He uses healing to give us a taste of His love, His abilities, and the overwhelming blessings He has in store for those who live for Him.

6. *God knows we will share our testimonies so others will believe.* We see this displayed throughout the Bible (e.g., Matthew 9:26; Matthew 9:31). This is also exactly what we are about to see when we read Lisa's miraculous testimony and see how it leads her to tell others about God:

So You Will Believe

As established earlier, we do not always have control over whether we need to be healed. There are also times when the need to be healed has nothing to do with our decisions; people may simply need God to heal them, so they will believe in Him. In John 9:1–12, Jesus said neither the man nor his parents had sinned, but he was born blind so the works of God might be displayed in him.

Remember Naaman and his healing from leprosy? After he was healed, he went back to Elisha, the prophet, to offer a gift of appreciation for the miracle he experienced. When Elisha refused the gift, Naaman responded by saying that he would never make burnt offerings and sacrifices to any other God but the Lord (2 Kings 5:17).

So Others Will Believe

God knows that miraculous healings will draw people's attention toward Him. He also knows healing one will pique the curiosity and interest of others, leading them to believe in Him. Luke 18:35–43 offers an example of how God will heal one so many will believe. There was a blind man who heard a crowd going by, and he asked what was happening. When they told him that Jesus was passing by, the blind man asked Jesus to have mercy on him. Jesus stopped and asked him what he wanted. The man asked to receive his sight, and Jesus restored it. Verse 43 says, *"…When all the people saw it, they also praised God."* While the man's request resulted in restoration of his sight, it also caused all the witnesses to praise God.

This was not the only account when a miraculous healing caused people to believe *and* acknowledge God's greatness. In Luke 7:11–17, Jesus raised a little boy from the dead. The scriptures say when the boy got up, the people were filled with awe and praised God. Mark 2:1–12 references Jesus forgiving the sins of a paralyzed man and ordering him to get up and walk. The passage says the miracle amazed everyone and they praised God because they had never seen anything like that.

Over and over again, the Bible shares stories of people being healed miraculously. Afterward, those healed and the witnesses turned to worship God, the source of all miraculous healings. Here are a couple more examples of healings that led to praising God:

- After a leper was healed by Jesus, he returned to praise God (Luke 17:15).

- Peter healed a lame beggar, who then praised God as onlookers filled with wonder and amazement at what God had done (Acts 3:6–10).

SKIN CELL REMOVAL TO HEART SURGERY

In 2003, I had a stent put in because I had a 70–80 percent blockage to my lungs. They put a stent in and said, "We want you to come back in a couple of years. We want to make sure everything is going well."

I hadn't planned to go back, but I did because I had a mass growing on my thigh. I went to the doctor and he said it was "no big deal. It's nothing to worry about." I received prayer for it and my pastor, Apostle Spearman, told me it's a mass of skin cells, so I didn't have to be afraid. Apostle told me to go to the doctor and have it removed.

I went to the doctor. He said they would do an outpatient procedure and I would be out of the hospital in a couple of days. I had it all set up. I called my mom and told her what was going on. She asked if there was any risk and asked what kind of anesthesia they were going to use. I told her I hadn't asked, but it would probably be a general anesthesia. She said I needed to give them my history and let them know about my heart before getting the anesthetic.

I told the doctor that I had been to the cardiologist. He told me they weren't going to put me under anesthesia without my cardiologist's approval. I didn't see the connection and thought it was ridiculous, but I went to the cardiologist.

The fifteen-minute appointment turned into two hours, as they discovered an 80 percent blockage in my artery, and blockage near my heart. After testing my blood pressure, it was 170/90. I felt fine, but the doctor said he would put me on blood pressure medicine. I told my husband, Jason, about it and he said, "We're going to believe God [will heal you]."

After going back for blood work, it turned out I needed heart surgery because of the blockage in the shunt and the overgrown scar tissue [from the 2003 procedure].

Two weeks before the surgery, Apostle Spearman called me and said, "We're going to pray for you." He told me God shared something with him that he needed to tell me. Apostle had never seen the pictures of how the scar tissue had grown, yet he described all that was in the picture. He and Prophetess Spearman, his wife, said the scar tissue was going to be stretched and straightened. I had no idea that it should have been stretched or straightened.

Once we got into the surgery, they had some issues with the balloon. They didn't have the right size yet, but the doctor said it stretched just right to fit that stent. The doctor was amazed at the stretching.

When Apostle said stretching before, we didn't know what he meant. But God knew what was going to happen.

I thought I was going to spend the night [at the hospital] but by 10 p.m. that night, they said I could go home!

While I was in recovery, I was coughing terribly, which resulted from the blood pressure pills I had taken. The doctor gave me some morphine to calm the cough so they could check the X-ray to see why I was coughing. The morning after recovery, the doctor came in and said I had hypertension and was going to be on blood pressure pills for the rest of my life. My blood pressure at that time went down to 162/84. They increased my medication and told me not to plan on getting off them.

I went for a two-week follow-up appointment. The doctor checked my blood pressure, left the room, and then sent the nurse in to check my pressure. I wondered why he sent the nurse. I prayed and was hoping it wasn't bad news.

The doctor said my blood pressure was 134/82! The doctor changed my dosage from every day to every other day.

People say they believe in miracles, but it's not until they've heard my whole story that they are shocked and now really believe in miracles.

Lisa Snider
Grand Rapids, Michigan

As Lisa shares her story with others about how God healed her heart, she helps to increase others' belief in God and encourages their belief in what He can do to help them. Lisa is doing what we saw Peter and John do in Acts 3:11–12 and 16, pointing people toward God. Our responsibility, after experiencing miracles, is to share with others what God has done. Much like these examples, our sharing will encourage others to believe in Him and, in turn, they will encourage others to do the same.

81

Chapter 8

Our Response To Miraculous Healings

A gain, God's intention for our lives is that we remain well. When He created mankind, He did so with the intent and desire that we would be healthy within our heart, soul, mind, and body. However, Adam and Eve chose to follow their own version of God's rule. This caused them, and all of us, to live with the consequences of the decision they made, requiring our need for restoration; thus, God sent His Son, Jesus, to take on the punishment for our sins, restoring our relationship with Him. This restoration leads to rejuvenation of our heart, soul, mind, and body, causing us to excitedly and willingly share with others our good news.

After being in that relationship with Billy, I thank God that I recognized His desire to have a relationship with me. I, in turn, began to follow Him; then, the healing process for my heart, mind, and soul began. By God's grace, I am now spiritually, mentally, emotionally, and physically whole. Believe me, I tell everyone who is willing to listen about how God took a girl who made a mess of her life and made it beautiful.

Just like with me, God desires a relationship with you. He wants to heal you fully, your whole being. He longs to spend time with you because He created you and loves you. Just as a parent desires a close relationship with their child, God desires a close relationship with you. Salvation, accepting God's deliverance from the penalty of sin, is the beginning of a personal relationship with God. This is what God wants for you so you can experience a life led by Him and His good intention.

Salvation and miraculous healings are two significant methods for God to get our attention. Once God has our attention, we will begin to recognize His overwhelmingly benevolent plans and abilities. Our natural inclination toward His undying love for us should be to love Him in return. Our response to experiencing salvation and miraculous healings should mimic that of Naaman, the blind beggar, the leper, and all the others. We should love and praise God while encouraging others to do the same.

God's miraculous healings should move our heart toward loving Him, as well as loving others. Our response to His healing should leave us no choice in the matter. Loving others helps us to forgive and care for

84

them, even when people blatantly mistreat us. Read how John experienced an amazing, miraculous healing that moved him to show love and forgiveness toward his very literal enemies:

DEAD AND READY TO RETALIATE

I got into an argument with three guys at a nightclub. It all started when a young lady came up to me and wanted to be my woman. It had something to do with prostitution (I had women out there for me). I told her no and gave her back to the guy she was trying to get away from. He got jealous. Things got heated and words were exchanged. I walked up to the guy and he tried to hit me. The other two guys that were with him ran to the door. The bouncer came over and told me I had to get out.

When I opened the door to leave the club, one of those other guys stabbed me in the shoulder. As that guy stabbed me in the shoulder, another guy stabbed me in the back; and another one stabbed me. Altogether, there were eleven stab wounds. They threw me in the trunk of a car, drove around, and put me in some bushes. A friend of mine found me pulling myself up on a telephone pole and rushed me to emergency. In the emergency room, the doctors said I died three times while they were working on me. By the third time, they put a tag on my toe and covered me up with a sheet. They were taking me to the morgue when my sister came in and started praying for me. [My sister said] while she was praying, I sat up while under that sheet!

While I was healing, I was wearing a catheter and a lung machine. They didn't think I was going to be able to make babies or that I would be able to use my right leg again. The stab wounds punctured my lungs, just missed my heart, just missed my spinal cord, punctured my bladder, punctured my rectum, and tore my kneecap. I was in the hospital for six months.

After I got out of the hospital, I started drinking a fifth of liquor a day. I started messing with marijuana, cocaine, and crack cocaine. I got to the point where I wanted to kill myself all over again. I started asking God why He let me live.

I asked the Lord to make me well enough to kill the people that stabbed me. They were going to die...by my hands. I didn't care about the circumstances.

As time went on, I kept asking God why He saved me. This went on for about twenty years. Then, about two years ago, I started getting answers. I'm just now today, from twenty years ago, starting to see what God's got for me.

To whom much is given, much is required. God's showing me some of the things He has for me. He [figuratively] gave me $10 and I jacked it up. He said if I can't give you $10, how could I give you $1 million. He's now given me ideas and promised me a whole lot of things.

God has opened my eyes to a whole lot of things. I see my wife now. I recently realized, "I'm married" [meaning he had to start acting like a husband]. I've been married twenty-eight years. It took me so long to figure that out because the devil had me so wrapped up in his darkness that I couldn't see. I was so confused because of the drinking and drugging.

God told me He would bring me through all the mess and when He did, He would help me forgive myself. He said He also needed me to forgive those guys. I told God that I did not want to forgive those guys. Overnight, He changed my heart!

I went to my pastors and I told them I needed to forgive those guys. The very next morning, a friend of mine said, "I've got a feeling you're just talking from the side of your neck." Later, we walked in the store and one of the guys that stabbed me, the ringleader, was there.

I walked up to him and shook his hand.

I guess God made it where he didn't think I was coming to retaliate. He just stood there like he couldn't move. I said, "I forgive you, my brother." That was from my full heart, and I walked out of there with tears in my eyes. The other two I haven't seen yet.

John Dandridge

What an incredible testimony of God's miraculous ability to heal John's heart, soul, mind, and body! His heart and soul were healed when he let go of his will and anger to receive God's will to forgive. His mind was healed, allowing him to begin to trust that God would bring him through the drugs and illicit lifestyle; also helping him to become conscious of being married. God definitely healed John's body when He raised John from the dead! God also allowed John's body to be restored from the tremendous damage of all the stab wounds. If you were to see John, you would have no idea that there was a possibility of him not using his right leg again. He was healed completely. God is truly a miracle worker!

John is not the first or the last whom God has brought back from the dead. There have been several accounts over the years of people sharing how they were dead but returned to life. God has been raising the dead for a long time. The Bible lists several accounts of people raised from the dead, both children and adults alike. Stories can be found in 1 Kings, 2 Kings, Luke, John, Matthew, Mark, and Acts. Since God controls all things in the physical and spiritual realms, it only makes sense that raising the dead is fully possible for Him.

We all love when miraculous healings happen for us or our family members. It helps us remember God's intention for our lives is that we all will be well (Exodus 23:25). However, there are times when God may not restore us to our originally intended state. For reasons we do not always understand, God may choose to withhold the experience of His miraculous healings. At times, He renders the doctors unable to find the cure. The therapist cannot reveal the source of the pain. The illness does not go away.

During moments where God withholds His healing, it is vital that we remember that He *still* loves us deeply. He is *still* very concerned about how we feel. He is *still* with us. He also wants us to *still* love Him. He wants us to remember and share with others all the *other* wonderful things He does for us.

Our daughter, Aniyah, enjoys eating snacks. She does not eat a lot of food at one time, so she is often found asking for a snack. Every now and then, we allow her to stay up later than her normal bedtime. When that happens, she usually wants a snack. She is a clever girl and has learned that if she asks for fresh fruit or veggies as a snack, I typically grant her wish. However, on those late nights, past her bedtime, I know it is not good for her to eat so close to going to sleep. And as expected, she asks for that snack, mainly a piece of fruit. I know she is a little hungry because she always is, and she is awake later than normal. I also know fruit is good for her. However, I tell her "no." She does not understand the importance of not eating so close to bedtime so she does not like my answer, but she has to trust my knowledge, my love for her well-being, and my intention to do what is best for her.

If you're a parent, teacher, or leader of any sort, you know you cannot give people everything they ask for, even if what they want is good, they really want it, and you really want to give it to them. There is more to consider than what you want to give them or what they really want. You have to consider all parties involved, the past, the present, and the impact on the future. God does the same for us. He considers the full situation, our requests, and the impact they will make on every individual's personal experiences for all generations to come after us; *then* He decides what is best. This can mean that it may be optimal for the situation to change *or* for the situation to stay the same.

Frankly speaking, we do not want to be the one whose situation does not change for the betterment of all generations to come. The truth is, there are not many who would voluntarily choose that position. Therefore, God has to allow circumstances to stay the same. Yet, He gives people the strength to endure, even though it grieves His heart to see His people suffer (Isaiah 41:10).

In the following testimony, we will see that God does not always heal those who want to be healed. Moreover, we will see that while God sustained Charnette long beyond what the doctors expected, she also loved and praised Him, without fail, in the midst of her illness. Ultimately, God allowed her to enter His presence and live a joyfully, healthy, eternal life with Him.

MULTIPLE MYELOMA

In 2003, I was working at a factory. I got to the point where I just couldn't work anymore. My shoulder would hurt so badly that I would cry while working. I had to quit my job because of the pain. When I left my job, I left my insurance behind. I was told to go to a free clinic because I had no money. The free clinic doctor told me, "You need to see a hematologist." I did not understand why. But knew I had no money for more tests and appointments, so I did not go.

After eight months, I went back to the free clinic and saw a new doctor. He asked why I did not go to the hematologist. I told him I had no money, so no one would see me. The doctor said I needed to see a hematologist so he could be 100 percent sure about my problem. Then he realized the previous doctor never shared the results with me. I told him the previous doctor would not tell me about the results until after I saw the hematologist, which I never did. The doctor looked at me and said, "Ms. Herring, you have cancer."

The doctor told me I would die in six to twelve months. I asked him what to do next. He said, "You don't understand what I'm telling you. There's no cure for multiple myeloma. What's going to happen is your bones are going to start breaking, and you will basically live in a bed. You won't be able to walk or pick up anything. The best thing we can do is keep you comfortable."

The doctor did not understand my focus on living when he told me I was dying. He thought I did not understand the results. He checked with Pastor Martha, who was with me, to see if I understood. I shared with the doctor the story in the Bible of the twelve spies. I told the doctor how ten of the spies went out and returned to the camp reporting fear of what was ahead in the Promised Land. The people in the camp believed them and cried all night. The other two spies were encouraged and ready to go into the Promised Land and fight. Everyone that listened to the ten and cried

91

all night died without going into the Promised Land. I made up my mind that I was not going to cry.

Because of my belief, the doctor started creating a plan. He suggested chemotherapy and radiation. He suggested a bone marrow transplant. He thought it could extend my life up to ten years. I rejected the transplant because I believed God would heal me.

Two years later, in 2005, I decided to tell my daughter about my diagnosis. I reassured her I would be fine. As I was leaving her house that day, I stepped off the porch and the bone in my right thigh broke. I had to have a steel rod placed in my leg. I later had to get another rod placed in my right shoulder because that bone had broken as well.

The doctor put a chemo board on my right side for transfusions. This caused me to have to learn to walk again. The whole process started over again on my left side.

This is what I have been told: there is no cure for multiple myeloma, and there is no medication that can cause you to live, not even chemotherapy. If you were to look up multiple myeloma, it would say you will probably die during your first round of chemotherapy, which means you will only live about six months. If you live through that one, you will go through another round of chemotherapy. You more than likely will not live past the second round. If you do, set your affairs in order because you will die. They will not give you a third round of chemotherapy. They consider it useless.

I've already gone through two rounds of chemotherapy. This is my third round of chemotherapy.

This is unusual. They usually say, "Go home and die." I refused to die because God said, "If you ask anything in Jesus' name, I will do it." We prayed and we asked the Father to save my life.

Charnette Herring (she lived until 2012)
Jenison, Michigan

Charnette was not cured of multiple myeloma, but she loved and appreciated God for allowing her to live almost ten years after her diagnosis with three rounds of chemotherapy and no bone marrow transfusion. Remember, the doctor said she would only live six to twelve months without the transfusion. She lived nine years without it! She loved and praised God until she died. She recognized that while God had not yet healed her of multiple myeloma, there were several other wonderful things He had done for her regularly. Like Charnette, we need to stay hopeful even when God does not do for us what we want Him to do.

Our ability to still love God when we are in pain can be a powerful encouragement for others. People may watch to see how we respond when God does not give us what we want. Others may be inspired by our patient hopefulness in spite of our situation. Still, others may be amazed at how we are able to maintain optimism and treat people kindly while we are facing adversity.

We know God's plan for our lives is for us to be well, but our inability to know everything depletes us of the understanding as to why He does and does not allow circumstances to be resolved. Therefore, it is best to remember that He loves us and we, in return, should remain full of expectation, trust, and love for Him.

Sometimes, though, the fact of the matter is, we may not receive healing at all. In 2 Corinthians 12:7–10, Paul had an ailment that brought discomfort. While Paul's ailment is undetermined, what we do know is Paul asked God to remove it, but God did not. Instead, God responded by saying that His grace was sufficient, and His power was made perfect in weakness. In this case, God chose not to heal Paul for reasons that Paul believed would keep him humble. Even though God did not heal Paul, he did not curse God, get angry, or stop doing the work he was doing for God. Instead, he said, *"That is why, for Christ's sake, I delight in weaknesses, in insults, in hardships, in persecutions, in difficulties. For when I am weak, then I am strong"* (2 Corinthians 12:10).

Also, 2 Corinthians 1:3-4 says to praise God, the Father of compassion, *"who comforts us in all our troubles, so that we can comfort those in any trouble with the comfort we ourselves have received from God."* It does not say He will remove all our troubles. It says when others are troubled, we will be able to give them the same comfort God has given us. In other words, use your experience to comfort and encourage others regardless of whether or not you receive the healing you want.

As a teenager, I often wondered why I went through the difficulties I experienced. I wondered why the abuse...the neglect...the drug and alcohol abuse...the legal trouble. I was not rescued from any of it. I was angry, frustrated, and deeply disappointed with my life.

In my early twenties, I became a youth development worker at a group home for teen girls and boys. As I listened to their stories, I realized I was not overwhelmed or shocked with what they shared. In fact, their stories were familiar. I was able to relate and encourage those youth in their situations, helping them to discover their ability to move forward successfully on their own path of life. I was proof that life's negative circumstances did not automatically equate to a lifestyle of poor choices and challenging situations.

Now that I have become a high school counselor, I am afforded even more opportunities to help students by listening to their difficulties, sharing my story, and helping them see that they are understood. I stand before them as an example, showing that they can go through their challenges and still become healthy, functioning adults. Although I was not delivered out of my past experiences, I am able to support and strengthen others because God comforted and encouraged me.

Again, God is all-knowing and perfect in His plan for our lives. Therefore, we can trust Him when He does not grant us certain desires of our heart. It is important not to lose focus of the fact that while God may not provide a particular type of healing for us, He has provided plenty of other experiences where we have been healed. He has also provided provision for us through food, clothing, shelter, people who care, doctors, jobs, etc. It is very easy to look past all that God has so graciously given to us throughout a single day or even over the span of our life and focus on the one thing He did not do. Let's do our best to change our focus, reflecting on what God has done instead of what He has not done. We will find we have a lot more to think on when we focus on that.

Chapter 9

Remember This

We have just witnessed how so many people have felt compelled to live out God's request to love Him, through their pain and healing. We have even witnessed people's love for God when their pain or sickness was not removed. If you or someone you know needs healing, it is most important to understand that God sees, knows, and cares. He may send healing and He may not. Either way, we have to trust that He knows all and is doing what is best for the eternal life of all mankind, a concept of which we cannot fathom.

If we happen to be one chosen to receive the blessing of a miraculous healing (beyond our daily miracles), we should always share our story to encourage others. We do not have to reveal the more intimate details, ensuring we are comfortable with what we share. However, we do need to share so we can help ourselves and others experience the full joy that comes from recognizing God's great work in our lives.

As you move forward on your journey in life, exploring more about who God is and what His requests are from you, I implore you to keep Psalm 107 on your mind. It shows how God is faithful and stands firm in His promises to His people. He is the Hero, Rescuer, and Savior of our lives because He said He would be:

Give thanks to the Lord, for he is good;
his love endures forever.
Let the redeemed of the Lord say this—
those he redeemed from the hand of the foe,
those he gathered from the lands,
from east and west, from north and south.

Some wandered in desert wastelands,
finding no way to a city where they could settle.
They were hungry and thirsty,
and their lives ebbed away.
Then they cried out to the Lord in their trouble,
and he delivered them from their distress.
He led them by a straight way
to a city where they could settle.
Let them give thanks to the Lord for his unfailing love
and his wonderful deeds for men,
for he satisfies the thirsty
and fills the hungry with good things.

Some sat in darkness and the deepest gloom,
prisoners suffering in iron chains,
for they had rebelled against the words of God
and despised the counsel of the Most High.
So he subjected them to bitter labor;
they stumbled, and there was no one to help.
Then they cried to the Lord in their trouble,
and he saved them from their distress.
He brought them out of darkness and the deepest gloom
and broke away their chains.
Let them give thanks to the Lord for his unfailing love
and his wonderful deeds for men,
for he breaks down gates of bronze
and cuts through bars of iron.

Some became fools through their rebellious ways
and suffered affliction because of their iniquities.
They loathed all food
and drew near the gates of death.
Then they cried to the Lord in their trouble.
and he saved them from their distress.
He sent forth his word and healed them;
he rescued them from the grave.
Let them give thanks to the Lord for his unfailing love
and his wonderful deeds for men.
Let them sacrifice thank offerings
and tell of his works with songs of joy.

Others went out on the sea in ships;
they were merchants on the mighty waters.

MIRACULOUS TESTIMONIES

They saw the works of the Lord,
his wonderful deeds in the deep.
For he spoke and stirred up a tempest
that lifted high the waves.
They mounted up to the heavens and went down to the
depths;
in their peril their courage melted away.
They reeled and staggered like drunken men;
they were at their wits' end.
Then they cried out to the Lord in their trouble,
and he brought them out of their distress.
He stilled the storm to a whisper;
the waves of the sea were hushed.
They were glad when it grew calm,
and he guided them to their desired haven.
Let them give thanks to the Lord for his unfailing love
and his wonderful deeds for men.
Let them exalt him in the assembly of the people
and praise him in the counsel of the elders.

He turned rivers into a desert,
flowing springs into thirsty ground,
and fruitful land into a salt waste,
because of the wickedness of those who lived there.
He turned the desert into pools of water
and the parched ground into flowing springs;
there he brought the hungry to live,
and they founded a city where they could settle.
They sowed fields and planted vineyards
that yielded a fruitful harvest;
He blessed them, and their numbers greatly increased,

and he did not let their herds diminish.

Then their numbers decreased, and they were humbled
by oppression, calamity and sorrow;
he who pours contempt on nobles
made them wander in a trackless waste.
But he lifted the needy out of their affliction
and increased their families like flocks.
The upright see and rejoice,
but all the wicked shut their mouths.

Whoever is wise, let him heed these things
and consider the great love of the Lord.

In the end, we can be sure that all God wants is for us to know how much He loves us. He knows all the wonderful blessings that come to those who love and believe in Him. It is out of His love for us that He looks for opportunities to bring healing, joy, and happiness to us all (Jeremiah 17:10). He may choose to bless us Himself or allow others to take part in His miraculous work. As we recognize God and His flawless handiwork in our lives, we will celebrate Him, enjoy our lives even more, and encourage others to do the same. May it all be well with you, and may you live a prosperous life!

If you would like to share your testimony, send comments about your experience reading *Miraculous Testimonies*, or request RaShonda to speak at your event, please send an email to jamersunpub@gmail.com.

Made in the USA
Middletown, DE
27 November 2022

15765569R00064